Human Rights

Critical World Issues

CRITICAL WORLD ISSUES

Human Rights

Brendan Finucane

MASON CREST
PHILADELPHIA

Mason Crest
450 Parkway Drive, Suite D
Broomall, PA 19008
www.masoncrest.com

Printed and bound in the United States of America.

CPSIA Compliance Information: Batch #CWI2016.
For further information, contact Mason Crest at 1-866-MCP-Book.

First printing
1 3 5 7 9 8 6 4 2

Library of Congress Cataloging-in-Publication Data

on file at the Library of Congress
ISBN: 978-1-4222-3657-4 (hc)
ISBN: 978-1-4222-8137-6 (ebook)

Critical World Issues series ISBN: 978-1-4222-3645-1

Table of Contents

KEY ICONS TO LOOK FOR:

Words to Understand: These words with their easy-to-understand definitions will increase the reader's understanding of the text, while building vocabulary skills.

Sidebars: This boxed material within the main text allows readers to build knowledge, gain insights, explore possibilities, and broaden their perspectives by weaving together additional information to provide realistic and holistic perspectives.

Research Projects: Readers are pointed toward areas of further inquiry connected to each chapter. Suggestions are provided for projects that encourage deeper research and analysis.

Text-Dependent Questions: These questions send the reader back to the text for more careful attention to the evidence presented there.

Series Glossary of Key Terms: This back-of-the book glossary contains terminology used throughout this series. Words found here increase the reader's ability to read and comprehend higher-level books and articles in this field.

What Are Human Rights?

Rigoberta Menchú was born in 1959, in a small village where everyone was very poor. She is a member of the Qiche, an *indigenous* tribe from Guatemala in Central America. Her father and her brothers were laborers on coffee and cotton plantations. The work was hard—15 hours a day— and two of her brothers died. One was poisoned by pesticide sprays and the other died from hunger. Rigoberta started work, aged 8, picking cotton. She had no chance to go to school.

The workers lived in crowded shacks, with no clean water or bathrooms. Often, all they had to eat was roots and leaves. Rigoberta's mother worked as a midwife, helping women and their babies. Many of them died, too, from poor food or disease.

Indigenous people made up two-thirds of the Guatemalan population, but they had no civil rights. The government and

In January 2011, thousands of Egyptians gathered in Cairo's Tahrir Square to demand political reforms. The protests, which soon spread throughout Egypt, forced longtime leader Hosni Mubarak to resign from office and leave the country. Unfortunately, the subsequent governments of Egypt have failed to deliver on the promise of greater freedoms and human rights for all Egyptians.

wealthy farmers took over their land. Rigoberta's father joined with other laborers to protest. They formed the United Peasant Committee, to organize petitions and demonstrations, asking for human rights. They were arrested and imprisoned many times.

Rigoberta and her brother Petrocino joined in the protests. In 1979, Petrocino was kidnapped, tortured, and burned alive. He was just 16 years old. The next year, her father and 38 other protest leaders died in a mysterious fire. Many people blamed the army for starting it. Rigoberta's mother was raped, then killed.

Rigoberta knew that her life was also in danger. In 1982,

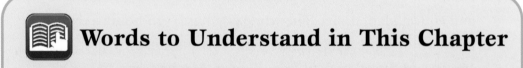

Words to Understand in This Chapter

asylum—a place of safety and refuge usually provided by a country for those seeking refugee status.

discrimination—the act of treating people worse because they belong to a particular group.

human rights—the rights that are regarded by most societies as belonging to everyone, such as the rights to freedom, justice, and equality.

indigenous—people who have lived in a country from earliest times, such as Australian Aborigines.

Nobel Peace Prize—a prize given as the highest international recognition to a person, or persons, for work contributing to peace, or the improvement of human rights.

racism—to discriminate against or attack a person, or a group of people, because of their skin color.

refugee—someone who is seeking safety, especially from war or persecution, by going to a foreign country.

Guatemalan activist Rigoberta Menchú speaks at a UN conference on Indigenous Peoples during 2014. Menchú is a human rights activist and Nobel Prize laureate.

she escaped across the border to Mexico. She decided to tell the world what had happened to her family and to all the other protesters, by writing a memoir. Her book *I, Rigoberta Menchú, an Indian Woman in Guatemala* was published in 1983. Her message was simple: "Native Americans are people and we want to be respected, not to be the victims of intolerance or racism."

After her book was published, Rigoberta dedicated the rest of her life to campaigning for human rights. She received the Nobel Peace Prize for her work in 1992. Rigoberta used her Nobel Prize money to fund an organization, named after her

This iconic image shows an unknown Chinese man standing in front of army tanks that are arriving to put down a human rights protest in Beijing's Tiananmen Square, June 1989. All around the world, men and women have risked their lives to stand up for human rights.

father. Today, that organization continues to work for indigenous peoples' rights all around the world.

What Are Human Rights?

The idea of human rights sets basic standards of justice, dignity, and respect for all humanity. It is closely linked to other important beliefs about how individuals should be treated and societies should be run, such as freedom, tolerance, and equal opportunities.

There are two different kinds of human rights. The first kind is things that people should be free to do, such as getting an education or taking part in politics. The second kind is things that people should be free from, such as discrimination or false imprisonment. Human rights belong to everyone, and cannot be taken away from any man, woman, or child. All human rights are equally important and are linked to each other. We cannot pick and choose between them.

In 1948 the United Nations, an organization of countries set up after the end of World War II to promote international peace and cooperation, issued a document called the Universal Declaration of Human Rights (UDHR). This was the first internationally agreed-upon statement related to human rights. It is still a very important document today.

The Declaration sets out 30 rights that people everywhere should be able to enjoy. These include life, liberty, and security—the basis for all other rights—plus freedom from slavery. It bans torture, as well as cruel, inhuman, or degrading punishments for prisoners. It states that everyone should have the right to a fair trial by impartial judges, and that people should not be unfairly arrested, detained, or exiled. Criminals should be presumed innocent until proven guilty. It also outlaws discrimination "of any kind, such as race, color, sex, language,

> "All human beings are born free and equal in dignity and rights. They are endowed [born with] reason and conscience and should act toward one another in a spirit of brotherhood."
>
> —Universal Declaration of Human Rights, 1948

Eleanor Roosevelt (standing) speaks to members of the UN committee that drafted the Universal Declaration of Human Rights. Roosevelt, the widow of the 32nd U.S. president, was a long-time campaigner for disadvantaged people. She headed the committee.

religion, political or other opinion, national or social origin, property, birth, or other status."

The Universal Declaration also says that governments should not interfere unfairly in people's lives, and that all men and women should have the right to be full citizens in the land where they were born. They should be able to travel, and to leave their country, and to seek asylum if they fear persecution. They should be free to marry, have a family, and own property. They should also be able to express their own religious beliefs and political ideas. They should be allowed to join together with others who hold similar views, and to take part in government. State-run services, such as schools and hospitals, should be open to all citizens, whatever their political or religious opinions.

Finally, the Universal Declaration sets out each individual's rights to seek work, to receive fair pay for their work, and to be given time off to rest and relax. It says that everyone should have the right to an adequate standard of living—that is, food, water, and shelter—and to receive benefits from state welfare systems, where they exist. It also stated that each person should have the right to an education, and should be permitted to take part in the cultural life of their community. (The full

Young Palestinians search through the rubble of their home, which was destroyed by Israeli airstrikes in Khuza'a, the southern part of the Gaza Strip. During the long-running conflict between Israel and the Palestinians, both sides have been guilty of human-rights abuses.

European Union vice president Catherine Ashton meets Soraya Rahim Sobhrang, an advocate for women's rights in Afghanistan.

text of the Universal Declaration of Human Rights is included as an appendix in the back of this book.)

Are Human Rights Popular?

Human rights involve many sensitive issues, such as race and religion. They affect all levels of society, from strong government leaders to people without power; such as homeless refugees. They give individuals the right to challenge national laws and state institutions, such as the army or the police. Sometimes, they can seem dangerous, or too "soft"—even murderers have human rights. For all these reasons, the issue of human rights can be controversial or deeply unpopular. Human rights organizations are often criticized by politicians and the media, and human rights campaigners are sometimes attacked.

This book will look at how and why the idea of human rights became increasingly powerful during the twentieth century, and at the role this idea plays in our world today. It will explore the way in which human rights—or the lack of them— have a big impact on all our everyday lives. It will also investigate how different individuals and organizations work to make sure that everyone, everywhere, can enjoy equal rights.

 **Text-Dependent Questions**

1. What message did Rigoberta Menchú express in her 1983 book?
2. In what year was the United Nations formed?
3. What are some reasons that the issue of human rights can be controversial or deeply unpopular?

 **Research Project**

Using the Internet or your school library, do some research to answer the question "Do Citizens have responsibilities in return for human rights?" One perspective is that people who are not good citizens do not deserve to have their rights protected. On the other hand, some believe that everyone should be entitled to human rights, however well or badly they behave. Present your conclusion in a two-page report, providing examples from your research that support your answer.

History of Human Rights

The idea of human rights as we understand it today is a relatively recent concept, emerging over the past three centuries. However, even ancient human societies had strong opinions about what "good" society should be like. In return for obeying the laws of ancient rulers, the people expected certain rights.

One of the oldest known legal codes dates from around 1790 BCE. It was made by Hammurabi, the king of Babylon, in the Middle East. Others ancient legal codes, such as the Jewish Ten Commandments (which were written down around 1000 BCE), the Hindu Vedas (from around 800 BCE) or the Sayings of the Chinese philosopher Confucius (from around 500 BCE), indicate that lawmakers from these times expected people to treat their fellow humans with dignity and to help needy mem-

The Code of Hammurabi was inscribed in the cuneiform script on a stone pillar. Hammurabi's laws formed the basis for government in the ancient Babylonian empire that he ruled, setting out the rights and duties of his subjects.

bers of their community. Many early societies had traditions such as the Jewish and Christian "golden rule," which stated: "Do unto others as you would have them do unto you." Similar teachings are found in the Christian New Testament, in which Jesus tells his followers to "Love your neighbor as yourself," and the Muslim holy book, the Qur'an.

Documents like the Magna Carta (1215 CE), drawn up as a result of a quarrel between King John of England and powerful people in his country, laid down some of the basic principles of modern human rights, such as the idea that even kings are not above the law. In 1776, the 13 American colonies issued a Declaration of Independence that stated, "all men are created equal." During the French Revolution, which began in 1789, antimonarchy protesters drew up a "Declaration of the Rights of Man and the Citizen." In 1848, over 200 women met at Seneca Falls, New York, to draw up a "bill of rights" detailing

 Words to Understand in This Chapter

communism—a system, or the belief in a system, in which capitalism is overthrown and control of wealth and property belongs to the state.

dictatorship—a country ruled by a person with absolute power.

guerrilla—a member of an unofficial military force, usually with some political aim such as the overthrow of a government.

persecute—to harass or treat badly.

Soviet Union—also known as the USSR (Union of Soviet Socialist Republics), a country formed from the territories of the Russian Empire in 1917, which lasted until 1991.

violation—an abuse of something, such as a person's human rights.

The Chinese philosopher Confucius taught that rulers had a responsibility to act in the best interests of their people, while the people had a responsibility to support and obey the ruler.

the social, civil, and religious rights of women. In 1863, President Abraham Lincoln issued the "Emancipation Proclamation," which declared African-American slaves to be "forever free."

Nations Come Together

During the early twentieth century, a succession of wars and revolutions made many people eager to develop international organizations that would work to reduce conflict and limit the harm done, especially to civilians.

In 1919, after the end of World War I, Britain, France, the

In 1215 King John signed the Magna Carta ("Great Charter"). It affirmed that the king, like everyone else, had to obey the law of the land. He couldn't exercise power arbitrarily. His subjects—at least those who weren't serfs—had rights and liberties.

United States, and their victorious allies organized an international peace conference in Paris. Delegates proposed that the defeated ruler of Germany, Kaiser Wilhelm II, be put on trial for a "supreme offense against international morality" for his role in bringing about war. This was the first time ever that a country's war-leader had been accused of such a crime.

The peace treaties signed at the end of the conference called for international protection for the rights of life, liberty, and freedom of religion. More importantly, they created the League of Nations, an organization that would work for international peace and cooperation. Among other things, it called for the fair treatment of ordinary people and it set up worldwide medical campaigns to end disease.

The League of Nations was a brave experiment, but it failed. Member nations refused to let international programs interfere with their own plans. This meant that the League was powerless against Nazi Germany, one of the most savage twentieth-century violators of human rights. After it came to power in 1933, the Nazi government began to exterminate men and

Members of the committee assigned to draft the Declaration of Independence—John Adams, Roger Sherman, Robert Livingston, Thomas Jefferson, and Benjamin Franklin— present the document to John Hancock, president of the Second Continental Congress, in June 1776. Written primarily by Jefferson, the Declaration of Independence carefully laid out the justification for the split with Great Britain. There were three essential parts. First, that all humans have certain fundamental rights. Second, governments are set up to protect these rights, and they rule only with the consent of the people. Third, when a government violates the people's fundamental rights, the people have the right to get rid of that government and create another.

women with mental or physical disabilities, and to persecute many minority groups, including Jews and gypsies. The League also failed to check aggressive actions by Japan and Italy during this time.

World War II began in 1939, with Britain, France, Russia, and later the United States, fighting against Nazi Germany and its allies. The war ended in 1945 but, long before that, the leaders of the Western democracies had declared their commitment to human rights. In 1941, U.S. President Franklin D. Roosevelt made a famous speech in which he declared that "Four Freedoms" were essential rights for all people, everywhere in the world: freedom of speech and religion, freedom from want, and freedom from fear.

Growing Awareness of Human Rights

When the war ended in 1945, the League of Nations was replaced by the United Nations (UN), an organization with greater authority to intervene in international affairs. In 1948, the United Nations issued a document called the Universal Declaration of Human Rights. Since then, human rights ideas have been encouraged in many different ways.

Some of the earliest and most successful human-rights campaigns were concerned with the right to "self-determination"—that is, to decide what the future of their nation should be. During the 1950s and 1960s, leaders of Asian and African countries began to demand independence from their European colonial rulers, such as Great Britain, France, the Netherlands, and Portugal. Fighting for greater rights helped many peoples to win independence from rule by stronger foreign countries—although their human rights aims were often mixed with the ambition for political power. For example, guerrillas in Malaya fought a long war against British colonial rulers from 1945 to 1957. They wanted political freedom, but once they gained it the leaders imposed a strict Communist rule, which often

High-ranking members of the Nazi Party and the German military are seated in court during their trial. After World War II ended in 1945, an international tribunal was set up to try German leaders accused of war crimes. This was one of the first-ever attempts by the international community to use the law to enforce human rights.

restricts the political rights of the people to participate in government or to protest against decisions.

As former colonies became independent, many of the leaders began their political careers by campaigning for human rights. For example, Nigerian activist Nnamdi Azikiwe organized local groups, calling for political, workers', or educational

In Poland during the 1980s, Lech Walesa led a labor union called Solidarity that helped bring an end to that country's repressive communist government.

rights, into a powerful National Council, which helped negotiate a new Nigerian Constitution with the British government. He became the first president of the independent republic of Nigeria in 1963.

Human rights ideas inspired some Communist nations in Eastern Europe to try to break free from domination by the Soviet Union and govern themselves. In 1977, a Czech protest group called Charter 77 began a long campaign for human rights. In 1989, Czech communist rulers were finally removed from power, and Vaclav Havel, the leader of Charter 77, became president of Czechoslovakia. Similarly, during the 1970s liberation movements in South America demanded freedom from dictatorship and called for international brotherhood.

In the United States during this time, there were numerous movements that were meant to deliver on the promise of the Declaration of Independence that all citizens should be treated equally. During the 1950s and 1960s, civil rights leaders in the United States, such as Dr. Martin Luther King Jr., called for an end to racial discrimination. Their work led to federal laws

African American civil rights leader Dr. Martin Luther King Jr. (1929–1968) once said, "Injustice anywhere is a threat to justice everywhere."

that made it illegal to prevent African Americans and other minority groups from voting, as well as programs that required public institutions to treat people equally regardless of their racial or ethnic background. From the 1960s to the 1990s, feminist movements campaigned for women's rights.

In the twenty-first century, gay pride campaigners have often linked their aims for personal freedom to wider issues of human rights. In June 2015, the U.S. Supreme Court ruled in *Obergefell v. Hodges* that states could not deny marriage licenses to same-sex couples, or refuse to acknowledge same-sex marriages performed in other jurisdictions. The Court found that such laws violated the Fourteenth Amendment to the U.S. Constitution, which said that all people must have equal protection under the law. Many other countries, including the United Kingdom, France, Norway, Brazil, Canada, South Africa, Argentina, and Uruguay, have also granted full rights to gay couples in recent years.

Present-Day Problems

Unfortunately, there are many places in the world where human rights are not respected. Today, one of the worst places is Syria, which has been engaged in a devastating civil war since 2011. For decades Syria has had a reputation as one of the most repressive dictatorships in the world. To date, the armed conflict in Syria has taken more than 220,000 lives and displaced more than 9 million people, roughly half of Syria's population.

Human-rights violations have been committed in Syria both by government forces and by rebel groups. A UN study found that all sides had engaged in acts that would be considered war crimes, including rape, murder, and torture. The Syrian government led by Bashar al-Assad has been condemned for using "barrel bombs"—improvised explosive devices dropped from helicopters—to devastate both civilian and rebel populations and turn Syria's once-proud cities into rubble.

Of all the various rebel factions fighting against the Assad regime, the most notorious is called the Islamic State of Iraq and the Levant (ISIL). By the summer of 2014 ISIL had gained control over more than one-third of Syria's territory, as well as large areas of neighboring Iraq. ISIL is a Muslim fundamentalist group that tortures and kills anyone who does not agree to its strict religious teachings, including Christians, Kurds, and Shiite Muslims living in territories it has captured. Other crimes include rapes and forced marriages, as well as the beheading of soldiers, journalists, and others captured by ISIL fighters. Because of this, the United States and other countries

A destroyed tank in front of a ruined mosque in Syria. The civil war in that country that began in 2011 has resulted in human-rights violations by nearly all the participants.

have been conducting airstrikes against ISIL positions in Syria and Iraq. Despite these attacks, ISIL had expanded into neighboring Lebanon, Jordan, and Libya by late 2015.

Another place where human-rights violations are common is in Israel, an important U.S. ally. This is due to a long-running conflict with the Palestinian Arabs that live in territories controlled by Israel since 1967: the West Bank, Gaza Strip, and Golan Heights. The Israeli government has allowed Israelis to construct settlements in the West Bank, which often results in fighting with the native Palestinians. Meanwhile, Hamas and other Palestinian armed groups in the Gaza Strip fire thousands of rockets and mortars each year toward Israeli cities and towns. Palestinian terrorist groups also launch rockets from neighboring countries like Lebanon and Syria, which have governments hostile to Israel. Israel's military typically responds with rockets, bombs, and artillery attacks of its own, which often devastate the civilian population centers from which Palestinian attacks come. In 2008–2009, 2012, and 2014 the

A young Syrian refugee in a camp on the border with Turkey. In March 2016, US Secretary of State John Kerry declared that one of the factions in the Syrian civil war, the Islamic State of Iraq and the Levant (ISIL), was carrying out genocide against Christians and other minorities in Syria.

Israeli military has sent tanks and troops into the Gaza Strip, resulting in thousands of Palestinian dead and wounded and the destruction of much of the region's infrastructure. Both sides in this conflict have been accused of violating the laws of war and of violating basic human rights.

In many other countries that are torn by conflict in 2016—Libya, Yemen, South Sudan, the Central African Republic, Mexico, and Pakistan, to name a few—human rights violations are common. Protecting human rights and enabling people to have a say in how their governments address their problems will be key to resolving disputes in these states.

 **Text-Dependent Questions**

1. What is the "golden rule?"
2. What did U.S. President Franklin D. Roosevelt declare in famous 1941 speech?
3. What was decided in the 2015 Supreme Court case *Obergefell v. Hodges*?

Research Project

Using the Internet or your school library, do some research to answer the question, "Should international organizations like the United Nations take action against countries to halt the abuse of human rights?" Some argue that the international community has a duty to protect human rights, and unless it acts many innocent people will be harmed. Others believe that foreigners should not interfere in any other country. Present your conclusion in a two-page report, providing examples from your research that support your answer.

How Can Human Rights Be Protected?

T he Universal Declaration of Human Rights describes human rights very clearly. But it is only a document, and by themselves words have no power: They need to be put into practice. How can this be done?

Governments can protect human rights in their national laws. This may mean amending old laws, or passing new ones. Governments can also sign legally binding documents, in which they promise to uphold human rights. These documents are called treaties or covenants. If a country signs a covenant, but does not follow it, other nations can take action, and even go to war, against the offending country.

Since 1948, when the Universal Declaration of Human Rights was released, its ideas have been included in two powerful international treaties: the International Covenant on

◀

American children examine the text of the Universal Declaration of Human Rights on December 10, 1950. The "December 10" date is set aside in every nation as "Human Rights Day," with programs held in schools and community centers to pay homage to the principles of freedom and the dignity of all people.

Civil and Political Rights (1966) and the International Covenant on Economic, Social, and Cultural Rights (1976). There are also more than 20 other treaties that are meant to protect the human rights of particular groups.

The United Nations

The United Nations (UN) can check how much each nation is doing to advance human rights. It can ask governments to submit regular reports, describing their past action on human rights and their plans for the future. The UN also listens to complaints of human rights abuses and it can send Special Representatives to human rights trouble-spots around the world.

Words to Understand in This Chapter

activist—someone who campaigns or works for a certain cause, such as human rights.

amend—to make changes to a text, in order to make it fairer or more up-to-date.

convention—an international treaty with the force of law.

covenant—a legally binding agreement; a treaty.

culture—the traditions/values, lifestyles, and beliefs shared by a group of people.

Islam—the religion of Muslims, who follow the teachings of the seventh-century Prophet Mohammed.

ratify—to sign or give formal consent to a treaty, contract, or agreement, making it official.

sanctions—measures taken against a country such as the stopping of trade.

tribunal—a temporary court, usually set up to hear a specific case, such as an allegation of racial discrimination.

A general view of participants during the 29th regular session of the Human Rights Council in July 2015.

In 2006, the United Nations Human Rights Council (UNHRC) was created. This organization includes representatives from 47 countries, and is responsible for promoting and protecting human rights around the world. The organization conducts a "Universal Periodic Review," which assesses the human-rights conditions in all 193 UN member states.

The United Nations has also set up intergovernmental organizations, such as UNICEF (the United Nations Children's Fund) and the World Health Organization (WHO), which work to improve human rights. They collect money, provide information, raise awareness, and send teams of experts to work in dangerous and difficult regions.

The UN Security Council is a group of 15 UN member states that respond to threats to world peace. This body has five permanent members: the United States, China, France, Great Britain, and Russia. The Security Council has the authority to establish international tribunals to prosecute crimes against human rights. It can even send peacekeeping troops to stop human rights abuses.

The United Nations often sends special representatives to visit countries that are engaged in civil wars. These representatives tour refugee camps and rough shelters to observe the conditions of children who had been driven out of their homes in the fighting. Such visits can put pressure on the national government to do all they can to make sure that children are given their human rights to food, shelter, education, and safety.

Unfortunately, the United Nations is sometimes accused of acting too slowly and too late. UN bureaucracy can take years to reach decisions, and sometimes gives in to pressure from powerful nations. For example, an official UN enquiry into the horrific genocide in Rwanda in 1994, when militias made up of the majority Hutu tribe killed over 800,000 members of the minority Tutsi tribe, found that the UN Secretary General "made weak and equivocal [uncertain] decisions in the face of mounting disaster." Also, the Security Council withdrew UN peace-keeping troops when it should have sent more, probably because of pressure from the United States and Belgium. It concluded that UN inaction had worsened the situation, and resulted in many Tutsi deaths.

(Top) Bodies of Rwandans killed during the genocide in 1994. Many of those who man-aged to survived the violence wound up living in crowded refugee camps (bottom).

In addition, the five permanent members of the UN Security Council can block proposals for actions if they are opposed to them for political reasons. As the Syrian crisis developed, Russia opposed a 2014 proposal that would have allowed the perpetrators of war crimes and human-rights abuses to be referred to the International Criminal Court, preventing it from going forward. Traditionally, Russia has been a strong ally of the Syrian dictatorship of Bashar al-Assad. In a similar way, the United States has typically shielded one of its closest allies, Israel, from Security Council actions, including a 2015 proposal by France that would have established a Palestinian state within two years.

People Power

Although they have no official status, individual human rights activists and non-governmental organizations, such as Amnesty International and Human Rights Watch, have probably done more than anyone else to improve human rights all around the world. They work by exposing human rights abuses, creating damaging publicity for abusers and campaigning for change. Compared with them, United Nations human rights organizations can often seem hesitant and slow.

In South Africa during the 1970s and 1980s, Bishop Desmond Tutu was the head of the Anglican Church. He constantly spoke out against the national system in which black South Africans were segregated from white South Africans, and treated as second-class citizens. This system was known as apartheid. He encouraged South Africans to take nonviolent action to end apartheid. He also encouraged the leaders of other countries to place sanctions on South Africa until it ended the apartheid system. When the apartheid system was finally ended in the early 1990s, Bishop Tutu was appointed to lead the Truth and Reconciliation Commission, which was formed to investigate human-rights abuses and help the country heal. For his tireless work, Tutu received the Nobel Peace Prize in 1984.

In the southeast Asian country of Myanmar (Burma), Aung San Suu Kyi was arrested in 1989 for campaigning against human rights abuses by the military dictatorship that seized power in the country. Over the next 21 years, she spent 15 years under arrest, making her one

Bishop Desmond Tutu speaks to the media about the apartheid situation in South Africa, 1985.

of the world's most prominent political prisoners. After she was released in 2010, she was finally able to receive the Nobel Peace Prize she had been awarded in 1991 for her work.

In recent years, Malala Yousafzai has become a hero to girls and women worldwide. She is an advocate for education and for greater opportunities for women in Muslim countries. Malala's family operates a school in the Swat valley of Pakistan. After an article she wrote for a newspaper, she became a well-known speaker on the subject of girls' right to

Aung San Suu Kyi spent many years in prison because of her opposition to the human-rights abuses committed by the military rulers of Myanmar.

education. In October 2012, the 14-year-old was shot by gunmen from the conservative Taliban movement, which wanted to prevent girls from going to school. Malala survived the attack and fled to England. She has continued to speak out on the importance of educating girls in Pakistan, and was awarded the Nobel Peace Prize in 2014.

Not Everyone Can Agree

The Universal Declaration of Human Rights aims to be "a common standard of achievement for all peoples and all nations."

Most countries have signed up to at least one of the many international treaties on human rights. However, not every country agrees to all of these treates. The United States and Somalia, for example, have not ratified a treaty called the Convention on the Rights of the Child.

There are several reasons why countries might not sign a human-rights treaty. Many governments see the UN's international covenants as a threat to their own independence. They do not want UN organizations, or foreign governments, interfering with their customs or their laws.

The leaders of some Asian or African nations view human

UN Secretary-General Ban Ki-moon meets with education advocate Malala Yousafzai (left), who in 2014 became the youngest recipient of the Nobel Peace Prize.

Bill Gates, founder of Microsoft, one of the richest companies in the world, has set up a foundation to help bring the human right of healthcare to people in developing countries. He is shown holding a dose of polio vaccine, while promoting a mass vaccination campaign. Vaccination is quick and simple, but it can prevent widespread suffering and save millions of children's lives.

rights covenants as the products of modern Western civilization. They believe the treaties are based on Western social, religious, and political ideas, which are alien to their cultures. Malaysia's Prime Minister argued that the Universal Declaration of Human Rights' emphasis on individual rights, rather than responsibility to the community, made it unsuited to Asia, where community relationships are seen as more important than individual rights. To solve this "culture clash," some nations have suggested alternative ways of advancing human rights, such as the Cairo Declaration on Human Rights in Islam, agreed by a group of Muslim states in 1990. This sets out rules to protect certain human rights, while also allowing for certain cultural practices and punishments that are specified in traditional Islamic religious laws.

In times of war or national emergency, many governments around the world tend to suspend human-rights protection in favor of greater security for the country. For example, after the September 11, 2001, terrorist attacks on the United States, the U.S. government arrested and imprisoned some Muslims sus-

Emergency responders view the aftermath of a terrorist bombing that killed 27 people at a synagogue in Istanbul, Turkey. Governments sometimes justify restricting the civil liberties of citizens in order to protect them from terrorism.

In London, crowds of protesters gathered outside the American embassy demanding the closure of the U.S. prison camp in Guantanamo Bay, Cuba. Human rights protesters have criticized the US government for locking up suspects here without trial. The controversial detention center for suspected terrorists was opened in 2002; as of 2015, more than 100 detainees remained at the facility.

pected of being involved in terrorist activities at the US naval base in Guantanamo Bay in Cuba. Their purpose was to detain suspected terrorists before they had a chance to commit any crimes. However, the administration of President George W. Bush authorized the use of torture in order to get information from these suspects. Also, these suspects were detained without trial for years, which violates an important right that is included in the Sixth Amendment to the U.S. Constitution.

The leaders of undemocratic government often oppose human rights legislation because they are frightened of losing power. They do not want to let ordinary people play a full part in government, or permit peaceable protests that might lead to a movement for change among their citizens. Communist countries like China tend to permit economic, social, and cultural rights while denying political rights. The Chinese government makes sure that most citizens have access to good healthcare and education, but punishes those who take part in political protests and may restrict peoples' right to travel abroad.

 Text-Dependent Questions

1. What UN organization was created in 2006 to protect human rights around the world?
2. What South African bishop helped to bring down the apartheid system?
3. What excuse to some governments use to suspend human-rights protection?

Research Project

Using the Internet or your school library, do some research to answer the question, "Is it ever appropriate to put people in prison before they have had a fair trial?" Those who believe the answer is yes will argue that sometimes, governments need to lock up people suspected of terrorism or other dangerous crimes in order to protect others from harm. Those who do not agree tend to believe it is a serious abuse of human rights to imprison people who have not been convicted of any crime. Present your conclusion in a two-page report, providing examples from your research that support your answer.

Helping People

Ideas about human rights can be powerful. They can give hope to people who are being wrongly treated. They can inspire people to work to make the world a better place, where there will be freedom, peace, and justice for everyone. Wherever we live, our lives are affected by ideas about human rights. If we live in a country that supports human rights, we have a much better chance of living the kind of life we want, in safety. If we live in a country where leaders ignore or oppose the idea of human rights, our lives will be restricted and possibly full of fear.

Human rights ideas can influence all aspects of our lives, even the most private. For example, in 2011 the United Nations Human Rights Council passed its first resolution recognizing LGBT (lesbian, gay, bisexual, and transgender) rights. The

People in Oakland, California, march to draw attention to the killings of several African Americans by police during 2014 as part of the Black Lives Matter campaign.

Council then issued a report that documented violations of the rights of LGBT people, including hate crimes, the criminalization of homosexuality, and discrimination. The Council encouraged all countries to enact laws protecting basic LGBT rights. Despite this, homosexual behavior is considered a crime in more than 70 countries, mostly in Asia and Africa.

Do Human Rights Help Workers?

UN conventions guarantee workers many different rights, including freedom from discrimination, fair working conditions, and the right to join workers' associations. They totally outlaw slavery or forced labor of any kind—of prisoners, for example, who may be made to work in prison in order to "qualify" for food. Some human rights campaigners also argue that workers should be free to refuse to work on projects—such as weapons manufacturing—that might be used to deny other peoples' human rights.

 Words to Understand in This Chapter

ethnic group—a group of people who share the same distinct culture, religion, way of life, or language.

forced labor—to make someone work, usually against their will, and under harsh conditions.

immigrant—someone who moves to and settles in another country.

microcredit scheme—a program of lending money at low interest rates to very poor people, who are not served by the big banks.

multinational—operating in many countries.

Members of a European trade union protest against policies of the European Union government in Belgium. Many countries protect the right of workers to form labor unions that will protect workers' rights.

UN covenants also require workers doing equal jobs to be given equal pay, and many nations have included these rules in their national law. Some countries, such as the United States, Australia, and the United Kingdom, have also established laws setting a minimum wage level. Workers who believe they are being paid unfairly can appeal to law courts or special tribunals to protect their rights.

Multinational corporations often look for the cheapest places to manufacture goods that will be sold worldwide. These businesses are not bound by any one nation's laws. Instead,

Women work in a small garment factory in Thailand. Some Asian countries rely so heavily on factories like these to earn export income, that they are unwilling to enforce laws meant to protect the rights of workers.

they seek to create the maximum profit for their shareholders. Sometimes, they deliberately place factories in countries where human rights laws are weak. They claim this gives the company greater flexibility. To help workers, some governments have tried to persuade corporations to obey laws protecting workers' rights by setting up groups such as the Apparel Industry Partnership. This is a group of American clothing manufacturers who agree to treat workers well. In return, they are more likely to win government contracts—and get good publicity.

The most successful campaigners for workers' rights have been non-governmental organizations that monitor worldwide labor conditions and report on them. Consumer groups have also been very effective—such as the American students who refused to buy their school and college wear from companies that treated their workers unfairly. The bad publicity that results from published reports on the sweatshop conditions that exist in the overseas factories of many well-known clothing or footwear companies have forced those companies to increase wages and improve working conditions.

Rights for Refugees

The Universal Declaration states that "everyone has a right to seek and to enjoy in other countries asylum from persecution." But this human right is often challenged by nations where refugees seek to settle, even when their governments have agreed to protect the rights of refugees and asylum seekers. For example, since the Syrian civil war began in 2011, more than 11 million people have been displaced from their homes. Over 4 million have fled the country, with many of these refugees living in camps in neighboring Jordan, Lebanon, Turkey, and Iraq. A growing number of Syrian refugees have sought refuge in Europe, and have risked a dangerous and illegal crossing of the Mediterranean Sea to get to Greece and Hungary. From there, they attempt to move to other European countries, hoping to build new lives.

Human rights groups have helped some refugees challenge government actions in court. But this is a slow and expensive process, and national laws are often carefully drafted to stay

Syrian refugees wait at the Keleti railway station in Budapest, Hungary, hoping for transportation to Germany, September 2015.

just within the provisions of the United Nations rules. Some European countries, such as Germany, are more willing to accept immigrants than others are.

The Syrian crisis aside, governments and politicians in wealthy countries are often unwilling to accept refugees because they believe most are not "in genuine need of asylum." They argue that they are "economic migrants" searching for work, and that they will be a burden on the host community. During the 2016 presidential campaign in the United States, for example, Republican candidate Donald Trump called for the mass deportation of undocumented immigrants from Mexico and Latin America.

Women and Children

Women make up the majority of the world's population, but nowhere are they completely equal with men. In Arab countries like Kuwait and Saudi Arabia, women do not have legal independence. In Thailand, Ukraine, and Moldova, young women are often forced to work in the sex industry. Millions

Officers with the U.S. Immigration and Customs Enforcement (ICE) agency arrest undocumented workers in Houston. They will be deported back to the Latin American country where they came from.

Women sell woven baskets at a market in Bangladesh. They were able to start their small business through a loan from the Grameen Bank, which pioneered the idea of microcredit in order to reduce poverty.

of women have been raped by soldiers in Syria, Sudan, and other war-torn places. Even in places like Europe and the United States, women are still often paid less than men for doing exactly the same job.

Most nations claim to value their young people, yet UN data shows that nearly 6 million children die before the age of five each year. The death rate for children in low-income countries of Africa and Asia is more than ten times as high as the death rate in the developed world. Children who survive into their teen years may be forced to work, beg, or serve as soldiers. Many face bullying, neglect, or sexual abuse.

In spite of these grim statistics, human rights advocates are helping to improve women's and children's lives. Powerful UN Committees can put pressure on governments by asking for reports on progress toward rights. For example, many countries have implemented new basic literacy programs for women, along with programs to help them find jobs, Microcredit schemes, which lend small amounts of money to very poor people, also enable women to help themselves out of poverty by giving them the means to create small businesses. In Brazil, the government has a program in which it gives money to poor

In some countries older people who can no longer work must resort to begging to survive.

families so their children do not have to drop out of school in order to work and help support their family. That way, the children get their human right to education, and with it the chance of a better future, but their families can still afford to buy food—another basic human right.

Despite these examples of progress, it has been difficult to persuade many traditional societies to give up customs that abuse women's and children's rights. When one Masai woman from Kenya took her husband to court for beating her so severely that she needed hospital treatment, she was supported by the Kenyan Branch of the International Federation of Women. Lawyers. They wanted the public to recognize that wife-beating was against human rights. The woman won her case, but now she says, "Women are very angry with me . . . it is unheard of in Masailand to put your husband into jail."

Rights for the Aged and Disabled

More than 600 million people all around the world live with a disability. Their experiences vary, but they all face some kind of discrimination, such as lack of employment opportunities. This is often caused by ignorance or prejudice. In many countries, people with disabilities are doubly disadvantaged. They share their fellow-citizens' problems of poverty or repressive government, while having to cope with extra difficulties caused by their disability as well. Old people, who are no longer fit and strong, often face similar discrimination.

The United Nations has been working to achieve human rights for people with disabilities since the 1980s, setting out various international rules intended to help bring about disability rights. In 2008, the UN Convention on the Rights of Persons with Disabilities was ratified and went into effect. To date 157 nations have agreed to this convention. The UN has also appointed a high-ranking official, called a Special Rapporteur, to monitor disability rights worldwide.

In some countries, disabled people are still treated as if they are less than human, and denied almost all rights. In 2002, for example, human rights campaigning group Amnesty International called for international protests against conditions in Bulgaria. There, people with mental or physical disabilities are shut away in homes and hospitals, described as

This disabled Sudanese man helps to make crutches, wheelchairs and special shoes for other persons with disabilities in the North Darfur region of Sudan.

"worse than prison." Some are forced to submit to treatment against their will; others die "as a result of gross neglect."

In 2010, the United Nations established the UN Open-ended Working Group on Ageing (OEWG), which was intended to strengthen the protection of older people's human rights. When the OEWG met in June 2015, it discussed proposals for a new international convention on older people's rights. The proposed convention would establish legal standards that challenge and replace stigmatizing attitudes and behavior related to age, and clarify how human rights apply in older age.

Human rights ideas have had a powerful impact. They have inspired many campaigners to argue that people with disabilities, and old people as well, are not people "in need," who should be helped for kindly or charitable reasons. Instead, they are people with just the same human rights as other members of society, whose rights—for example, to work, to suitable housing, or to travel—are often rationed or denied.

 "Older persons are the custodians [keepers] of our traditions, our heritage, and our cultures. They reflect our past and are mirrors of our future. They have the right to a healthy, productive life, to live in a caring environment, and to be treated with respect"

—Zola Skweyiya, former Minister of Social Development in South Africa

Justice and Human Rights

The Universal Declaration of Human Rights states that "All are equal before the law," and that every person is entitled to a

Human rights activists participate in a demonstration to protest against the Chinese government's repressive policies toward Uyghurs, an ethnic minority that mostly lives in the Xinjiang region of northwestern China.

Russian police scuffle with protesters during a rally in central Moscow. Human rights protesters have criticized the Russian government for quashing dissent and locking up those who disagree with the regime's policies without fair trials.

fair trial. It adds that no person should be arrested without reasonable suspicion that he or she committed a criminal act, and that every person should be presumed innocent until they are proven to have committed a crime.

It is every government's duty to ensure law and order for the benefit of all citizens, but this cannot be imposed at the expense of the basic rights of the people. Without a fair system of justice to regulate society, there can be no human rights.

Laws set standards for the protection of human rights in each country. The national justice system—including judges, police, and public officials—make sure that laws are obeyed. If there are unjust laws, or corrupt judges and officials, then human rights are likely to be ignored.

In countries with violent or repressive rulers, judges, police, and court officials are themselves often accused of human rights crimes. Often the armed forces are involved as well. Sometimes, human rights violations happen when a government feels that it is facing an emergency, such as a sudden rise in crime. Sometimes, they are used as a brutal way of silencing the opposition, and staying in power.

Human rights organizations keep a careful lookout for human rights crimes. For example, in 2014 the killing of an African-American teenager, Michael Brown, by a police officer in Ferguson, Missouri, led to riots and drew national attention to the issue. Thanks to the Twitter app, the hashtag #BlackLivesMatter became instantly popular. As other police shootings of unarmed African Americans have been reported, the Black Lives Matter movement has resulted in marches and protests in many cities.

Careful monitoring and international appeals cannot force any government to change its behavior, but they can bring unwelcome publicity, and encourage respect for human rights. Organizations like Amnesty International USA have supported such appeals. "The tragedies of Michael Brown [and others] impact all of us, everywhere, because everyone has the human right to life and to be safe in our communities, and to be free from discrimination and when these rights are not protected,

Protesters march against police shootings and racism during a rally in Washington, D.C., during December 2014.

our communities become locked in fear and polarized," said Amnesty International worker Muhammad Malik. "Mothers and fathers live in constant fear that what should ordinarily just be a walk in the park for their child might transform into a moment of brutal state violence. Communities lose faith in their judicial system and that lack of trust can lead to a sense of nihilism and depression that saps communities and undermines civic engagement. . . . Amnesty International supports an independent, impartial investigation of the death of Michael Brown and of the apparently heavy-handed tactics used by police in the aftermath of Michael's death."

The situation facing minorities in the United States, particularly African Americans, in prison is also grim. Today, there are more prisoners, in more crowded prisons, than ever before. Attacks by warders or other prisoners are common, and conditions are dirty and unsanitary. Human Rights Watch, a campaigning organization that monitors conditions in prisons, commented, "We believe that a government's claim to respect human rights should be assessed ... by how it treats its prisoners, including those not held for political reasons."

Enforcing Antidiscrimination Laws

Many countries have passed laws incorporating the Universal Declaration's ban on "discrimination of any kind." Yet despite this, discrimination on grounds of race, caste, tribe, religion, and many other causes, is still widespread.

The United Nations has the power to examine each member nation's laws, to make sure that they do not violate human rights. For example, the UN has declared that it is "concerned ... that the [laws] of Yemen did not contain explicit provisions [clear rules] prohibiting discrimination on the grounds of race or ethnic origin." In Senegal, it recommended that the government take action "to promote understanding, tolerance, and friendship among racial and ethnic groups." However, it can often be difficult to make nations accept criticism and improve human rights.

Many nations now have independent "watchdogs" to mon-

An Australian demonstrator holds a placard outside a courthouse in Melbourne.

itor the impact of their antidiscrimination laws, such as the Human Rights Bureau in the US Department of State, or the Commission for Racial Equality in the United Kingdom. Campaigning groups have set up international networks, such as UNITED, in Europe, which has 450 member organizations in 43 countries, and links with over 1,000 similar organizations worldwide. There are even special campaigning groups dedicated to checking sites on the Internet, since communication via the Web makes it much easier for racists to spread their anti-human rights message and escape antidiscrimination laws.

 **Text-Dependent Questions**

1. What are some rights guaranteed to workers by UN conventions?
2. How many people have been displaced since the Syrian civil war began in 2011?
3. In what year was the UN Convention on the Rights of Persons with Disabilities ratified?

Research Project

Using the Internet or your school library, do some research to answer the question, "Do countries have a moral duty to accept refugees who have been driven from their homes by war?" On one hand, these people have been caught up in terrible circumstances through no fault of their own, and they deserve help. However, many people believe that it is difficult enough to provide food, shelter, and jobs for all of a country's own citizens, without having to provide aid for asylum seekers as well. . Present your conclusion in a two-page report, providing examples from your research that support your answer.

Defending Human Rights

T he Universal Declaration of Human Rights states that all "individuals, groups, and organs of society" have a duty to encourage human rights. In practice, human rights action is often left to a few brave individuals, such as Rigoberta Menchú or Malala Yousafzai, or to dedicated non-governmental organizations like Amnesty International and Human Rights Watch. Many democratic countries have government agencies that are involved in protecting human rights, and of course the United Nations itself is very concerned with human rights. However, getting all of these agencies to agree on a course of action, or to work together, can seem like an impossible task.

The international media plays an important part in safeguarding and promoting human rights. It does this in several

Former soccer star David Beckham, a UNICEF Goodwill Ambassador, meets with a seven-year-old fan during a program for young people. Goodwill Ambassadors help to raise awareness of human-rights issues.

ways. Journalists have the skills to investigate human rights abuses that have been deliberately concealed. They can give publicity to human, rights campaigners, and help them win more supporters. They can subject human rights abusers to hostile questioning, and expose them to criticism and contempt from people all around the world. However, this work is not without danger, and many journalists and other media workers, such as photographers, are killed or threatened each year.

Famous public figures can also help to promote and defend human rights, by bringing publicity and encouraging public support. For example, UNICEF (the United Nations Children's Fund) regularly appoints well-known people, such as singer Katy Perry and tennis star Serena Williams, to serve as special ambassadors. UNICEF sends these special ambassadors to visit areas where it is working for children's rights. In recent years celebrities like Angelina Jolie, George Clooney, and Bono have drawn international attention by becoming involved in campaigns to protect the rights of poor people in developing countries or countries threatened by repressive regimes.

Respected religious leaders, such as the Buddhist Dalai Lama and the Roman Catholic Pope Francis, have seen it as

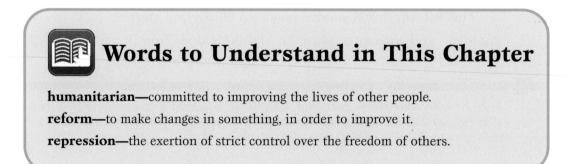

Words to Understand in This Chapter

humanitarian—committed to improving the lives of other people.
reform—to make changes in something, in order to improve it.
repression—the exertion of strict control over the freedom of others.

Amnesty International members participate in a Gay Pride parade in Paris.

their duty to use their influence to campaign for human rights, especially religious freedom and respect for indigenous cultures. "Religious freedom is not just a matter of thought or private devotion," Pope Francis said at a conference in Rome in June 2014. "It is the freedom to live—both privately and publicly—according to the ethical principles that are a consequence of the truth found."

Punishing Those Who Violate Human Rights

In democratic countries where there are fair and honest laws, people who feel deprived of their human rights can take

Religious leaders like the Roman Catholic Pope Francis often use their positions to advocate for greater respect for human rights.

employers, organizations, or even governments to court. But in wartime, or in countries with repressive governments, this is not possible. It can also be very difficult for people in one country to take action against human rights abusers in another land.

However, there are ways to take action. During the 1970s and 1980s, many nations, companies and individual consumers took part in a boycott of South African goods to protest against the apartheid system. They refused to buy South African goods or sell aircraft and weapons to South Africa's armed forces until the system was abolished.

Trade arrangements have also been used to put pressure on governments with poor human rights records. Since the 1970s, the United States has restricted trade to certain countries with repressive governments. These include Iran, Lebanon, Libya, North Korea, Somalia, Sudan, and Syria—all of which are infamous for human-rights violations. Of course, the U.S. does allow trade to other countries that are known to allow human-rights abuses. China is one of the largest U.S. trade partners, for example, while Saudi Arabia and Israel are important allies in the unstable Middle East region.

One of the most powerful "weapons" in the fight for human rights is collective action by groups of nations. They can force all their members to accept human rights as a condition of joining their group. For example, the country of Turkey has been trying to join the European Union since the late 1980s. However, its application has stalled in part because leaders of the EU believed that the Turkish government did not safeguard the rights of its citizens. In 2013, for example, the Turkish police cracked down hard on anti-government protestors, killing 11 people and injuring more than 8,000. In response, the German government blocked

 "You can intimidate the prisoner; you can frighten the immigrant; you can silence the refugee, but we will not be intimidated and we will not be frightened and we will not be silenced. We will stand up for freedom and security and human rights. And we will prevail."

—William F. Schulz, former executive director of Amnesty International USA

The headquarters of the European Union in Brussels, Belgium. Countries that wish to join the European Union must agree to support human rights ideals, and to introduce human rights policies into their laws.

Turkey's application from proceeding. Actions like this can persuade governments that are not eager supporters of human rights to improve their citizens' lives. They see agreeing to human rights as a fair price to pay for the political and economic benefits that belonging to the larger group will bring.

Does International Aid Make a Difference?

International aid can also be used to fight for human rights. For example, in the late 1990s in East Timor, the Indonesian army and police took no action when armed gangs attacked civilians who had voted for independence. The killings prompted a forceful letter, threatening to withdraw aid, from the president of the World Bank, which had loaned the Indonesian government vast sums of money. The president wrote: "For the international financial community to be able to continue its full support, it is critical that you act swiftly to restore order and that your government carry out its public commitment to honor the referendum outcome."

Another example is Myanmar (Burma), where a military junta seized power in 1989. The The country was isolated by

An oil refinery in the Arabian desert. Saudi Arabia is the world's largest supplier of oil. Its wealth gives it the power to choose whether or not to abide by human rights laws.

international sanctions until it made a transition to a civilian government in 2011. The new government soon made substantial reforms intended to protect human rights. It began to release political prisoners such as Aung San Suu Kyi. In response, the international community withdrew the sanctions. President Barack Obama became the first American president to visit the country in 2012, and the resumption of international aid and trade helped Myanmar's economy grow at a strong 8 percent rate in 2013 and 2014.

There are many kinds of freedom—from the personal to the

A member of the European Union visits a health clinic in Yangon, Myanmar. In 2012 the EU announced a $150 million assistance package to support democratic reforms and development in the country.

political—protected by the Universal Declaration for Human Rights. These include freedom to choose a marriage partner, freedom of thought, conscience, and religion, freedom to speak a local language, and freedom to elect a government. Because "freedom" can mean so many things, it is often difficult to enforce by law.

Legal Recourse

There are legal ways to punish human rights abusers, even at a distance. For example, the European Court of Justice has the power to try all alleged breaches of European Union law, including human rights crimes. Citizens of many EU member nations have challenged their own governments' actions in the court, and many have won. This court works because EU member states recognize its authority.

During the 1990s, to punish human rights abusers in Rwanda and the former Yugoslavia, the United Nations established temporary special courts called tribunals. These were used to hold trials for army leaders and soldiers accused of war crimes. The tribunals were effective because they were backed up by the threat of military action, and economic sanctions as well.

After 1945, an International Court of Justice was established at The Hague in the Netherlands. It is part of the United Nations, with judges from many nations elected by the Security Council and the General Assembly, but its main concern is to settle disputes between UN member nations. In July 2002, a permanent International Criminal Court (ICC) was created. Its purpose was to investigate and bring to justice indi-

Judges of the International Court of Justice (ICJ) hear a dispute between two countries. The court meets in The Hague, Netherlands.

viduals who commit genocide, crimes against humanity, and war crimes when the justice systems of individual states cannot or will not prosecute those offenses. Through 2015, thirty-six people had been indicted by the ICC, although many of these cases are still pending.

Sometimes, the human right to freedom of speech can seem very uncomfortable. For example, a well-known French historian denied that the Holocaust (the deliberate massacre of millions of Jews by German Nazis during World War II) had taken place. The government of France threatened to prosecute him for racial and religious discrimination. In return, he accused the French government of abusing his human right to free speech. However, the European Human Rights Commission ruled that the French government had been correct. It said that the right to freedom of speech does exist, but that a person could not use his free speech rights to used to violate other human rights, such as freedom from discrimination.

Finally, human rights abusers can often be made to reform once they realize that it is in their own interest to do so. This was summed up very well by American Secretary of State Cyrus Vance, speaking in 1977. "We seek these [human rights] goals because they are right—and because we, too, will benefit. Our own well-being, and even our security, are enhanced in a world that shares common freedoms and in which prosperity and economic justice create the conditions for peace.

> According to the Committee to Protect Journalists, each year around 45 to 60 journalists and other media workers are killed worldwide because of their work. In 2015, Syria, South Sudan, Yemen, and Mexico were among the most dangerous countries in which to be a journalist.

Why Doesn't Everyone Enjoy the Same Rights?

In spite of hard work by the United Nations, and by many individuals, governments, and campaigning organizations, millions of people still do not have basic human rights. Sometimes, powerful people do not want to give others equality, justice, or free-

Russian police detain a gay rights activist who was participating in an unauthorized gay pride parade in Moscow.

dom, usually for political reasons. For example, in 2012 Russia passed a law that required non-governmental organizations such as Human Rights Watch and Amnesty International to register as "foreign agents," effectively labeling them as spies. Under President Vladimir Putin, Russia tolerates no opposition and crushes any criticism. Those who speak out against the Putin regime, such as activist Alexi Navalny, are often arrested on weak or trumped-up charges.

Often, governments let commercial or political interests affect their view of civil rights issues. They will turn a blind eye to human rights abuses in countries that are political allies, or trading partners. For example, Israel and Saudi Arabia are strong allies of the United States. Both countries have been regularly cited by international organizations, including the United Nations, for human-rights abuses and repression, but the US government rarely rebukes these strategic allies.

Sometimes, shortages of information prevent people from understanding the idea of human rights. For many years, China prevented foreigners from visiting Tibet, which its army occupied in 1950. Chinese rulers in Tibet made efforts to

Human rights activists protest outside the Saudi Arabian embassy in Oslo, Norway, to demand the release of an imprisoned Saudi blogger, Raif Badawi, in May 2015.

South Sudanese journalists attend a four-day workshop aimed at discussing and highlighting issues on the promotion and protection of human rights in media coverage, media laws, and the safety and security of journalists in South Sudan. The workshop was organized by the Human Rights Division of the UN Mission in South Sudan (UNMISS), UN Educational, Scientific and Cultural Organization (UNESCO), Albany Associates Ltd., and the Union of Journalists in South Sudan.

destroy traditional Tibetan culture and replace them with Chinese ideas—a clear breach of Tibetan peoples' human rights. But until outsiders knew what was happening within Tibet, they were powerless to act.

Sometimes, people facing problems do not think human rights could help them. A children's charity worker explains that in traditional societies, parents don't see the point of send-

ing children with disabilities to school. But by denying these children their right to an education, these parents are limiting their children's lives.

Supporters of human rights are often not free to act exactly as they would like. Individual human rights campaigners do not have much power when faced with hostile governments, and they are often short of money to finance their protests. Many humanitarian organizations deliberately do not protest about lack of human rights, for fear of offending governments in countries where they work. They concentrate on practical projects, such as healthcare or feeding schemes, and this work saves millions of lives.

Sometimes, human rights organizations simply make the wrong decisions, or fail to achieve what they set out to do. For example, the United Nations has sent peacekeeping troops to many countries in an attempt to end civil wars or avoid a human-rights crisis. Unfortunately, some of these peacekeeping efforts do not succeed. In places like Somalia (1992), Bosnia and Herzogevenia (1995), and Rwanda (1995), as well as in numerous African countries during the twenty-first century, UN peacekeepers have been forced to retreat, having failed in their mission.

Bringing Freedom

The idea of human rights can set standards to aim for, and they inspire courage and hope. For example, women forced by family pressure to marry against their will can appeal to women's groups who work to support human rights. Even though these groups cannot change traditional attitudes, they can provide information, counseling, and legal advice—and possibly a safe place to hide.

On some occasions, human rights ideas can help bring a complete change of policy. This has happened in many remote European regions, where people have increasingly claimed the right to speak local languages as part of a wider campaign to be free from central government control. In Scotland and Ireland, for example, at one time the native Gaelic language was banned in government schools, and children who spoke it were beaten. Today, Gaelic is taught in many Scottish and Irish schools, and there are government-sponsored newspapers, television, and radio stations created specially for Gaelic-speakers.

 # Text-Dependent Questions

1. What are two ways that famous public figures can promote and defend human rights?
2. What countries has the United States restricted trade with because of their human-rights abuses?
3. How many people have been indicted by the International Criminal Court?

Research Project

Using the Internet or your school library, do some research to answer the question "Should governments support human rights even if doing so damages their economic Interests?" Supporters of this view would argue that an individuals human rights should be more important than money. Opponents would say that a government has been established to make the entire community prosperous and safe, and that the rights of society are more important than the rights of an individual. Present your conclusion in a two-page report, providing examples from your research that support your answer.

The Universal Declaration of Human Rights, 1948

Whereas recognition of the inherent dignity and of the equal and inalienable rights of all members of the human family is the foundation of freedom, justice, and peace in the world,

Whereas disregard and contempt for human rights have resulted in barbarous acts which have outraged the conscience of mankind, and the advent of a world in which human beings shall enjoy freedom of speech and belief and freedom from fear and want has been proclaimed as the highest aspiration of the common people,

Whereas it is essential, if man is not to be compelled to have recourse, as a last resort, to rebellion against tyranny and oppression, that human rights should be protected by the rule of law,

Some members of the U.N. Commission on Human Rights rehearse for a television program, "You and Human Rights," broadcast on CBS in 1949. Pictured are (left to right) E. Kelen of the U.N. Radio Division, Professor Rene Cassin of France, Dr. P.C. Chang of Chinal, CBS network moderator Quincy How, Human Rights Commission chairperson Eleanor Roosevelt of the United States, and Dr. Charles Malik of Lebanon

Whereas it is essential to promote the development of friendly relations between nations,

Whereas the peoples of the United Nations have in the Charter reaffirmed their faith in fundamental human rights, in the dignity and worth of the human person and in the equal rights of men and women and have determined to promote social progress and better standards of life in larger freedom,

Whereas Member States have pledged themselves to achieve, in cooperation with the United Nations, the promotion of universal respect for and observance of human rights and fundamental freedoms,

Whereas a common understanding of these rights and freedoms is of the greatest importance for the full realization of this pledge,

Now, therefore, The General Assembly, Proclaims this Universal Declaration of 'Human Rights as a common standard of achievement for all peoples and all nations, to the end that every individual and every organ of society, keeping this Declaration constantly in mind, shall strive by teaching and education to promote respect for these rights and freedoms and by progressive measures, national and international, to secure their universal and effective recognition and observance, both among the peoples of Member States themselves and among the peoples of territories under their jurisdiction.

Article 1

All human beings are born free and equal in dignity and rights. They are endowed with reason and conscience and should act toward one another in a spirit of brotherhood.

Article 2

Everyone is entitled to all the rights and freedoms set forth in this Declaration, without distinction of any kind, such as race, color, sex, language, religion, political or other opinion, national or social origin, property, birth, or other status. Furthermore, no distinction shall be made on the basis of the political, jurisdictional or international status of the country or territory to which a person belongs, whether it be independent, trust, non-self-governing or under any other limitation of sovereignty.

Article 3

Everyone has the right to life, liberty, and security of person.

Article 4

No one shall be held in slavery or servitude; slavery and the slave trade shall be prohibited in all their forms.

Article 5

No one shall be subjected to torture or to cruel, inhuman, or degrading treatment or punishment.

Article 6

Everyone has the right to recognition everywhere as a person before the law.

Article 7

All are equal before the law and are entitled without any discrimination to equal protection of the law. All are entitled to equal protection against any discrimination in violation of this Declaration and against any incitement to such discrimination.

Article 8

Everyone has the right to an effective remedy by the competent national tribunals for acts violating the fundamental rights granted him by the constitution or by law.

Article 9

No one shall be subjected to arbitrary arrest, detention, or exile.

Article 10

Everyone is entitled in full equality to a fair and public hearing by an independent and impartial tribunal, in the determination of his rights and obligations and of any criminal charge against him.

Article 11

1. Everyone charged with a penal offense has the right to be presumed innocent until proven guilty according to law in a public trial at which he has had all the guarantees necessary for his defense.

2. No one shall be held guilty of any penal offense on account of any act or omission which did not constitute a penal offence, under national or international law, at the time when it was committed. Nor shall a heavier penalty be imposed than the one that was applicable at the time the penal offense was committed.

Article 12

No one shall be subjected to arbitrary interference with his privacy, family, home, or correspondence, nor to attacks upon his honor and reputation. Everyone has the right to the protection of the law against such interference or attacks.

Article 13

1. Everyone has the right to freedom of movement and residence within the borders of each State.

2. Everyone has the right to leave any country, including his own, and to return to his country.

Article 14

1. Everyone has the right to seek and to enjoy in other countries asylum from persecution.

2. This right may not be invoked in the case of prosecutions genuinely arising from nonpolitical crimes or from acts contrary to the purposes and principles of the United Nations.

Article 15

1. Everyone has the right to a nationality.

2. No one shall be arbitrarily deprived of his nationality nor denied the right to change his nationality.

Article 16

1. Men and women of full age, without any limitation due to race, nationality, or religion, have the right to marry and to found a family. They are entitled to equal rights as to marriage, during marriage, and at its dissolution.

2. Marriage shall be entered into only with the free and full consent of the intending spouses.

3. The family is the natural and fundamental group unit of society and is entitled to protection by society and the State.

Article 17

1. Everyone has the right to own property alone as well as in association with others.

2. No one shall be arbitrarily deprived of his property.

Joachim Rücker, president of the UN Human Rights Council, speaks during a March 2015 meeting in Geneva, Switzerland.

Article 18

Everyone has the right to freedom of thought, conscience, and religion; this right includes freedom to change his religion or belief, and freedom, either alone or in community with others-and in public or private to manifest his religion or belief in teaching, practice, worship, and observance.

Article 19

Everyone has the right to freedom of opinion and expression; this right includes freedom to hold opinions without interference and to seek, receive, and impart information and ideas through any media and regardless of frontiers.

Article 20

1. Everyone has the right to freedom of peaceful assembly and association.

2. No one may be compelled to belong to an association.

Article 21

1. Everyone has the right to take part in the government of his country, directly or through freely chosen representatives.

2. Everyone has the right to equal access to public service in his country.

3. The will of the people shall be the basis of the authority of government; this will shall be expressed in periodic and genuine elections which shall be by universal and equal suffrage and shall be held by secret vote or by equivalent free voting procedures.

Article 22

Everyone, as a member of society, has the right to social security and is entitled to realization, through national effort and international cooperation and in accordance with the organization and resources of each State, of the economic, social, and cultural rights indispensable for his dignity and the free development of his personality.

Article 23

1. Everyone has the right to work, to free choice of employment, to just and favorable conditions of work, and to protection against unemployment.

2. Everyone, without any discrimination, has the right to equal pay for equal work.

3. Everyone who works has the right to just and favorable remuneration ensuring for himself and his family an existence worthy of human dignity, and supplemented, if necessary, by other means of social protection.

4. Everyone has the right to form and to join trade unions for the protection of his interests.

Article 24

Everyone has the right to rest and leisure, including reasonable limitation of working hours and periodic vacations with pay.

Article 25

1. Everyone has the right to a standard of living adequate for the health and well-being of himself and of his family,

including food, clothing, housing, and medical care and necessary social services, and the right to security in the event of unemployment, sickness, disability, widowhood, old age, or other lack of livelihood in circumstances beyond his control.

2. Motherhood and childhood are entitled to special care and assistance. All children, whether born in or out of wedlock, shall enjoy the same social protection.

Article 26

1. Everyone has the right to education. Education shall be free, at least in the elementary and fundamental stages. Elementary education shall be compulsory. Technical and professional education shall be made generally available and higher education shall be equally accessible to all on the basis of merit.

2. Education shall be directed to the full development of the human personality and to the strengthening of respect for human rights and fundamental freedoms. It shall promote understanding, tolerance, and friendship among all nations, racial, or religious groups, and shall further the activities of the United Nations for the maintenance of peace.

3. Parents have a prior right to choose the kind of education that shall be given to their children.

Article 27

1. Everyone has the right freely to participate in the cultural life of the community, to enjoy the arts, and to share in scientific advancement and its benefits.

2. Everyone has the right to the protection of the moral and

material interests resulting from any scientific, literary, or artistic production of which he is the author.

Article 28

Everyone is entitled to a social and international order in which the rights and freedoms set forth in this Declaration can be fully realized.

Article 29

1. Everyone has duties to the community in which alone the free and full development of his personality is possible.

2. In the exercise of his rights and freedoms, everyone shall be subject only to such: limitations as are determined by law solely for the purpose of securing due recognition and respect for the rights and freedoms of others and of meeting the just requirements of morality, public order, and the general welfare in a democratic society.

3. These rights and freedoms may in no case be exercised contrary to the purposes and principles of the United Nations.

Article 30

Nothing in this Declaration may be interpreted as implying for any State, group, or person any right to engage in any activity or to perform any act aimed at the destruction of any of the rights and freedoms set forth herein.

Appendix

Joint Statement of the Chairpersons of the UN Human Rights Treaty Bodies on the Post-2015 Development Agenda

A s Chairpersons of the ten UN Human Rights Treaty Bodies, we recognize the fundamental importance of the current discussions on the post-2015 development agenda. We recall that the 2005 World Summit acknowledged that peace and security, development, and human rights are the three pillars of the United Nations system and recognised that "development, peace and security and human rights are interlinked and mutually reinforcing." We believe that the human rights treaty bodies have an important role to play in contributing to both the finalization and implementation of the post-2015 development agenda.

We recall our previous statement of May 2013, and recognize the progress since made, including the integration of important human rights elements in the Open Working Group's 17 draft Sustainable Development Goals (SDGs) and

169 targets, as well as the emphasis placed on human rights in the Secretary-General's synthesis report of December 2014 'The Road to Dignity: Ending Poverty, Transforming All lives and Protecting the Planet.' We believe that this provides a basis for a new and effective universal development agenda grounded in freedom from fear and freedom from want for all, without discrimination.

The emphasis placed by the Open-Working Group and the Secretary-General's reports on equality and non-discrimination, including two dedicated equality goals on gender equality and equality within and between countries, is crucial. Previous development efforts failed to produce sufficient improvements in the plight of the marginalized, disempowered and excluded, including women, children, minorities, indigenous peoples, migrants, older persons, persons with disabilities and the poor. Even where overall progress was positive, inequalities and inter-sectional discrimination have dramatically increased between social groups, countries and between regions. The inclusion of non-discrimination and social cohesion targets is, therefore, an important step towards a development agenda that leaves no-one behind.

We strongly urge Member States to maintain - and, indeed, strengthen - consistent alignment with, and references to, human rights, by recognising and including, inter alia:

- That in addition to economic and social rights, the inclusion of civil and political rights is a significant step towards a balanced and transformative agenda that addresses freedom from fear along with freedom from want. In this context, the reference to fundamental freedoms should be strengthened by explicitly referring to freedoms of expression, association and peaceful assembly (Goal 16, target 16.10) and the protection against torture, abuse, exploitation and trafficking should be expanded to cover adults, in addition to children (Goal 16, target 16.2).

- While the inclusion of the protection of fundamental rights and freedoms and promotion of gender equality in the goals and targets is crucial, this must reflect international human rights standards and not be limited by national laws (goals 5 and 16).

- While the explicit references to indigenous peoples in relation to food productivity (Goal 2, target 2.3) and universal access to education (Goal 4, target 4.5) are welcome, we propose the inclusion of the right to free, prior and informed consent of indigenous peoples in relation to decisions that affect them as a key means of ensuring respect for all rights and freedoms of indigenous peoples.

- Universal access to sexual and reproductive health services and reproductive rights is an important element of ensuring rights-based development, gender equality and empowerment of women and girls (Goal 5, target 5.6); we encourage an explicit reference to 'sexual and reproductive health and rights' that is fully consistent with international standards and the respect of the right of all women and girls, freely and without coercion, violence or discrimination, to have control over and make decisions concerning their own sexuality, including their sexual and reproductive health.

- Consideration should be given to the inclusion within the goals of universal implementation of accessibility and the application of reasonable accommodation the full exercise of the rights of persons with disabilities, including their effective participation in society.

- That goal 16, target 7 should be understood as including women, children, minorities, indigenous peoples, migrants, older persons, persons with disabilities and the poor.

- That goal 10, target 7 should be understood as encouraging respect for the human rights of migrants, regardless of their condition or status and preserving their human dignity.

- That goal 16, target 5 should stress that the elimination of corruption is essential to good governance, which is, in turn, a necessary condition for the full enjoyment of human rights.

- That in Goal 8 reference be made to the need for human rights-based protection of marginalized and disadvantaged groups, such as minorities, migrants or persons with disabilities, during economic downturns.

Members of the UN Human Rights Council hear a report on the situation in Syria, June 2015.

In this context, we strongly support the Secretary-General's calling on Member States to include a 'technical review' of the goals and targets in order to ensure that they are ambitious whist also measurable, achievable and consistent with existing international standards and agreements, including human rights treaties.

We welcome the emphasis placed on accountability and call for this to be strengthened. We strongly agree with the Secretary-General's call for a 'robust and participatory monitoring and review framework' for the SDGs at the national, regional and global levels, with a systematic and institutionalized flow of information from and to existing monitoring mechanisms, including the human rights treaty bodies, in order to ensure synergies between existing mechanisms and a post-2015 monitoring and review framework.

In this regard, we further believe that Member States should build upon the principles and inclusive working methods of existing mechanisms such as the Human Rights Treaty Bodies, as well as the Universal Periodic Review of the UN Human Rights Council.

Bearing in mind the many gains which are to be drawn from harnessing the energy and resources of the private sector to ensure the successful implementation of the SDGs, accountability mechanisms should also include accountability of the private sector. We underline the relevance of the work of the human rights treaty bodies in the area of corporate sector accountability and call upon Member States to endorse the call for the full application of the United Nations' Guiding Principles on Business and Human Rights, as referred to in the Secretary-General's Synthesis report.

We emphasize that measuring progress in achieving development goals should include an assessment of the contribution of such measurement processes to the protection of fundamental rights and freedoms. In addition, we stress the need for reliable and validated means of measuring progress in meeting development goals. Indicators should be based upon appropriately disaggregated data, derived from, and taking account of, new technologies.

In our own work, we will encourage our Committees to consider the impact of development goals on the enjoyment of the rights in our respective treaties. We will also encourage the Committees to draw on development data and reports, as appropriate, in our Committees' constructive dialogue with States.

The importance of a successful conclusion to this agenda-setting process cannot be underestimated. We encourage Member States and all stakeholders during these last stages of the intergovernmental negotiations to rise to the challenge of adopting a truly transformative, universal, and human rights-based development agenda that protects human dignity and contributes to the realization of human rights for all without discrimination.

—January 18, 2015

International Organizations

United Nations High Commissioner for Human Rights
Administrative Section
Office of the United Nations
High Commissioner for Human Rights
Palais des Nations
CH-1211 Geneva 10, Switzerland
Phone: +41 22 917 90 20
E-mail: InfoDesk@ohchr.org
Website: http://www.ohchr.org/english

Amnesty International
5 Penn Plaza
14th Floor
New York, NY 10001
Phone: (212) 807-8400
E-mail: aimember@aiusa.org
Website: http://www.amnestyusa.org

Human Rights Watch
350 Fifth Ave.
34th Floor
New York, NY 10118-3299
Phone: (212) 290-4700
E-mail: hrwnyc@hrw.org
Website: http://www.hrw.org

The Abolish Slavery Coalition

8620 W Third St.
Los Angeles, CA 90048
E-mail: richard@abolishslavery.org
Website: http://www.abolishslavery.org

African Commission on Human and Peoples' Rights

31 Bijilo Annex Layout, Kombo North District
Western Region P.O. Box 673 Banjul
The Gambia
Phone: (220) 441 05 05
E-mail: au-banjul@africa-union.org
Website: http://www.achpr.org

Series Glossary

apartheid—literally meaning "apartness," the political policies of the South African government from 1948 until the early 1990s designed to keep peoples segregated based on their color.

BCE and CE—alternatives to the traditional Western designation of calendar eras, which used the birth of Jesus as a dividing line. BCE stands for "Before the Common Era," and is equivalent to BC ("Before Christ"). Dates labeled CE, or "Common Era," are equivalent to *Anno Domini* (AD, or "the Year of Our Lord").

colony—a country or region ruled by another country.

democracy—a country in which the people can vote to choose those who govern them.

detention center—a place where people claiming asylum and refugee status are held while their case is investigated.

ethnic cleansing—an attempt to rid a country or region of a particular ethnic group. The term was first used to describe the attempt by Serb nationalists to rid Bosnia of Muslims.

house arrest—to be detained in your own home, rather than in prison, under the constant watch of police or other government forces, such as the army.

reformist—a person who wants to improve a country or an institution, such as the police force, by ridding it of abuses or faults.

republic—a country without a king or queen, such as the US.

United Nations—an international organization set up after the end of World War II to promote peace and co-operation throughout the world. Its predecessor was the League of Nations.

UN Security Council—the permanent committee of the United Nations that oversees its peacekeeping operations around the world.

World Bank—an international financial organization, connected to the United Nations. It is the largest source of financial aid to developing countries.

World War I—A war fought in Europe from 1914 to 1918, in which an alliance of nations that included Great Britain, France, Russia, Italy, and the United States defeated the alliance of Germany, Austria-Hungary, the Ottoman Empire, and Bulgaria.

World War II—A war fought in Europe, Africa, and Asia from 1939 to 1945, in which the Allied Powers (the United States, Great Britain, France, the Soviet Union, and China) worked together to defeat the Axis Powers (Germany, Italy, and Japan).

Further Reading

Alston, Philip, and Ryan Goodman. *International Human Rights*. New York: Oxford University Press, 2013.

Baughan, Brian. *Human Rights in Africa*. Philadelphia: Mason Crest, 2014.

Donnelly, Jack. *Universal Human Rights in Theory and Practice*. Ithaca, N.Y.: Cornell University Press, 2013.

Freeman, Michael. *Human Rights: An Interdisciplinary Approach*. 2nd ed. Cambridge, UK: Polity Press, 2011.

Goodhart, Michael. *Human Rights: Politics and Practice*. 2nd ed. New York: Oxford University Press, 2013.

Hunt, Lynn. *Inventing Human Rights: A History*. New York: W.W. Norton, 2007.

Rotberg, Robert I. *Transformative Political Leadership: Making a Difference in the Developing World*. Chicago: University of Chicago Press, 2012.

Smith, Rhona K.M. *Textbook on International Human Rights*. 6th ed. New York: Oxford University Press, 2014.

Yousafzai, Malala, and Patricia McCormick. *I Am Malala: How One Girl Stood Up for Education and Changed the World*. Boston: Little, Brown Books for Young Readers, 2014.

Internet Resources

http://www.hrw.org/en/africa
> The organization Human Rights Watch provides reports on human rights issues around the world. Each country also has its own page on this site.

http://www.amnesty.org
> Home page of the human rights organization Amnesty International, which includes links to reports and news updates related to every country.

http://www.abolishslavery.org
> Website of the Abolish Slavery Coalition, a group devoted to eradicating slavery and human trafficking worldwide.

http://www.un.org/en/rights/index.shtml
> The United Nations page related to human rights includes links to UN reports and agencies, as well as an online version of the Universal Declaration of Human Rights.

http://www.freedomhouse.org
> Freedom House is an independent watchdog organization dedicated to the expansion of freedom around the world. It rates the "progress and decline of political rights and civil liberties" in countries throughout the world.

http://www.child-soldiers.org

The home page of this group serves as an introduction to the countries where children are recruited as soldiers.

www.unhcr.org

Official site of the United Nations High Commissioner for Refugees. The website has texts of all human rights treaties and details of UN proceedings (committee meetings, press briefings, etc).

http://www1.umn.edu/humanrts

The University of Minnesota Human Rights Library is a massive resource, with over 65,000 documents related to human rights, as well as links to other websites.

Index

Numbers in **bold italics** refer to captions.

text of the, 83–92
and trials, 56
See also United Nations

Vance, Cyrus, 75

Walesa, Lech, *24*
Wilhelm II (Kaiser), 20
Williams, Serena, 66
World Health Organization
    (WHO), 33–34
World War I, 19–20
World War II, 21–22, *23*

Yousafzai, Malala, 37–38, *39*, 65

About the Author

Brendan Finucane studied history at Britain's Cambridge University and worked with Amnesty International. This is his first book for young people.